Chinese For Young Beginners 1 Workbook

By

Bill Li

Cover Illustrations by Candace Tong-Li

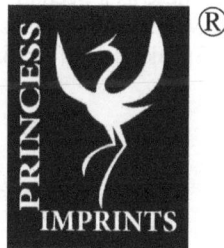

PRINCESS IMPRINTS ®

New York

Imagine. Create. Contribute.

www.PrincessImprints.com

Editor's Words

The Chinese for Young Beginners™ Courses and English-Chinese Bilingual Textbooks are designed to serve the special needs of children learning Chinese as a Foreign Language. With a *New Words and Expressions* table before each lesson as a reference tool, students can review and preview each lesson, as well as work on homework assignments without parents' help at home. The substantial game oriented exercises following each lesson not only allow teachers to engage students in fun activities, but also provide them a consistent underlying structure for comprehensive reviews.

Nurturing curiosity and encouraging creativity in learning is the core of our teaching approaches. We've intentionally kept a lot of white spaces throughout the books for young students to take notes, copy Chinese characters, make sentences, or draw pictures. We hope that young artist-writer Candace Tong-Li's enchanting illustrations will ignite young readers' own imagination and creative expression. We want to make learning Chinese a fun experience.

Chinese for Young Beginners 1 Workbook serves two purposes: (1) to reinforce learners' memory of vocabulary, sentence patterns, and language usages within context through repeated patterns of exercises, and (2) to help teachers evaluate student achievement upon completing *Chinese for Young Beginners 1* and readiness for *Chinese for Young Beginners 2*.

-- Ying Tong

1. Chinese Workbook for Children 2. Learning Chinese as a Second Language 3. Learning Chinese as a Foreign Language 4. Foreign Language Study/Chinese 5. Mandarin 6. Chinese 7. Beginners Chinese 8. Learn Chinese 9. Chinese Exercises 10. Chinese for Non-native Speakers 11. Teaching Chinese 12. Chinese Language Program

ISBN: 978-0-9854789-4-0

Bill Li
Chinese for Young Beginners 1 Workbook/Bill Li; Cover Illustrations by Candace Tong-Li
Princess Imprints, New York, 09/25/2013

www.PrincessImprints.com
Imagine. Create. Contribute.
Printed and Manufactured in the United States of America

Chinese For Young Beginners 1 Workbook

第一课 数一数

复习 (Review)

1. Count the following numbers in Chinese.

一 二 三 四 五
六 七 八 九 十
十 九 八 七 六
五 四 三 二 一

2. Rank the following in descending order:

六只狗　　七只狗　　一只狗

八只狗　　两只狗

三只狗　　四只狗　　九只狗　　五只狗

十只狗

3. Circle the correct number from the given numbers.

1) 五

   3   6   1   8   9   7   5   2   4   10

2) 一

   7   4   5   2   1   6   10   9   8   3

3) 八

   8   9   5   3   1   6   4   10   2   7

4) 九

   2   9   8   7   5   3   1   6   4   10

5) 七

   9   8   5   1   7   6   4   10   2   3

6) 四

2　9　4　5　1　6　7　3　8　10

7) 三

8　3　7　5　6　4　10　2　9　1

8) 十

9　6　10　1　7　2　3　4　5　8

9) 二

5　1　7　2　6　10　4　3　8　9

10) 六

9　6　3　5　1　7　8　4　10　2

4. Count up from 1 to 10; count down from 10 to 1; and, randomly count the numbers.

一二三四五六七八九十

十九八七六五四三二一

四十六一五三九七八二

5. Match the following Chinese to their corresponding pinyin.

七	wǔ
九	sì
三	liù
二	shí
五	sān
八	èr
四	jiǔ
十	qī
一	yī
六	bā

测验 (Quiz)

1. Write the numbers in Chinese in the exact order shown below. (30 pts)

10	2	9	8	3	4	1	7	6	5

2. Write pinyin in the parentheses. (20 pts)

一 (   )

二 (   )

三 (   )

四 (   )

五 (   )

六 (   )

七　　　　　（　　　　　　）

八　　　　　（　　　　　　）

九　　　　　（　　　　　　）

十　　　　　（　　　　　　）

3. Fill in the corresponding numbers in Chinese. (20 pts)

♥♥♥　　　　　　　　　　（　　　　　　　　）

♥♥ ♥♥　　　　　　　　　（　　　　　　　　）

♥♥♥ ♥♥♥♥　　　　　　　（　　　　　　　　）

♥♥ ♥♥ ♥♥　　　　　　　 （　　　　　　　　）

♥♥♥ ♥♥♥ ♥♥♥　　　　　 （　　　　　　　　）

♥♥ ♥♥♥♥ ♥　　　　　　　（　　　　　　　　）

♥♥♥♥♥　　　　　　　　　（　　　　　　　　）

♥♥♥♥♥ ♥♥♥♥♥　　　　　 （　　　　　　　　）

♥♥　　　　　　　　　　　（　　　　　　　　）

♥　　　　　　　　　　　 （　　　　　　　　）

4. Write your answers in Chinese in the boxes. (20 pts)

1) Nine birds are sitting on a tree, three flew away, how many birds are left now?

☐

2) Robyn has ten books. Her friend Sam borrowed seven books from her, how many books does Robyn have now?

☐

3) Mom went to Starbucks and bought three cups of coffee. While walking out of the store, she got a call from Dad who asked her to buy six more. How many cups of coffees did Mom buy all together?

☐

5. Count the squares below, and fill in the numbers in Chinese. (10 pts)

☐☐☐☐   ☐☐

(   ) + (   ) = (   )

第二课 我有一只黑的猫，你呢？

复习 (Review)

1. Fill in the following blanks with 有 or 没有.

1) 我_____一只白的狗，你呢？(have)
我_____。(do not have)

2) 我_____白的猫 (do not have)，我_____黑的猫。(have)

3) 我_____三个苹果，你_____几个苹果？
(have)
我_____苹果。(do not have)

2. Fill in the blanks with 也 or 还.

Note: "也" and "还" both can mean "also" but their usages are different. When using "也", you refer to the same objects or people; with "还", you refer to different objects; "还" implies "but also", "in addition".

Example 1: 我有一个苹果，我弟弟也有一个苹果。

Example 2: 我有一个红苹果，我还有三个绿苹果。

1) 我有一只黑的猫，我＿＿＿有一只白的狗。

2) 你有一只红苹果，我＿＿＿有一只红苹果。

3) 我有两个绿苹果，我＿＿＿有三个红苹果。

4) 你叫Sam，我＿＿＿叫Sam。

3. Fill in the blanks with the color words in Chinese.

1) 我有三个＿＿＿＿＿(red)苹果。

2) 你有没有_____(green)苹果呢？

  我没有。我有三个_____(yellow)苹 果。

3) 我有一只_____(black)的猫，你呢？

  我没有。我有一只_____(white)的狗。

4. Fill in the blanks with number, color and measure words in Chinese.

1) Mom bought three green apples, four yellow apples, and seven red apples.   My brother Andrew ate one yellow and one red apples, I ate two red and three green apples. How many apples are left now by color?

_____(green)

_____(yellow)

_____(red)

2) On Friday afternoon, I usually walk dogs for my neighbors. Sam has three dogs: one brown, one black, and one white; Robyn has two dogs: one black, one white; Jennifer has two dogs: one white and one brown; but Adam has only one black dog.

How many dogs do I have to walk on Friday?

_____(yellow)

_____(blue)

_____(white)

_____(brown)

_____(black)

_____(Total)

测验 (Quiz)

1. Write down the Chinese words you hear from the teacher. You can find the recording at www.PrincessImprints.com: Audio. (20 pts)

_____

_____

_____

_____

_____

_____

_____

_____

_____

2. Write the numbers in Chinese in the exact same order shown below. (20 pts)

7	3	5	10	2	9	8	1	4	6

3. Fill in the following blanks with 也 or 还.

(10 pts)

1) 我有两个绿苹果，我＿＿＿有两个红苹果。

2) 我有五个红苹果，我弟弟＿＿＿有五个红苹果，我＿＿＿有七个绿苹果。

4. Fill in the boxes with number, color and measure words in Chinese. (20 pts)

On the way home from school yesterday, the first three cars I saw passing by were two red, one white; the second three cars were one gray, one blue and one black; the last four cars were one yellow, one green, one red and one purple. How many cars did I see by color? The measure word for cars is "辆" (liàng). For example, "一辆黄的".

_____(red)

_____(white)

_____(gray)

_____(blue)

_____(black)

_____(yellow)

_____(green)

_____(purple)

5. Fill in the following blanks with 有 or 没有. (10 pts)

1) 我_____三个绿苹果 (have), 我弟弟

_____绿苹果。(does not have)

2) 弟弟_____一只猫(has)，我_____。(do not have)。

3) Sam_____狗，_____猫。(has neither)

6. Match the following Chinese to their corresponding pinyin. (20 pts)

一只黑的狗	nǐ yǒu hēi de gǒu ma
两只白的猫	yī zhī hēi de gǒu
三个红苹果	wǒ méi yǒu hēi de gǒu
四个绿苹果	sān gè hóng píng guǒ
我没有黑的狗	liǎng zhī bái de māo
我没有狗没有猫	wǒ yǒu qī zhī huī de māo
你有黑的狗吗	sì gè lǜ píng guǒ
我有七只灰的猫	wǒ méi yǒu gǒu méi yǒu māo

第三课 这是什么？

复习 (Review)

1. Fill in the blanks in Chinese.

1) 这是什么？

这是_____(one pencil)。

2) 我有_____(nine black pencils), 你呢？

_____(I don't have)。

3) 那是什么？

那是_____(three keys)。

4)弟弟有五支蓝的铅笔, _____
_____ (I also have five blue pencils. In addition, I have two red pencils)。

2. Fill in the blanks with appropriate measure words using 个 块 支 把 只.

1) 我有三__铅笔，弟弟一__铅笔也没有。

2) 我有两__咖啡的书包，弟弟有两__红的书包。

3) 这__钥匙是你的吗?

不，这__钥匙不是我的。

4) 这__黑板是我弟弟的，那__白板是我的。

5) 你有几__红苹果?
我没有红苹果。我有五__绿苹果。

6) 我有三__狗，你呢?

3. Negate the following sentences using 不，这不是.......

1) 这是一把钥匙吗?

_____。

2) 这是一个蓝的书包吗?

_____。

3) 这是一只黑的狗吗?

_____。

4) 这是一块白板吗?

_____。

4. Use 这是…… 吗？ to turn the following sentences into questions.

1) 这是一把钥匙。

_____?

2) 这是一只黑的狗。

_____?

3) 这是一支铅笔。

_____?

这是一块黑板。

_____?

这是一个灯。

_____?

测验 (Quiz)

1. Write the numbers in Chinese in the exact same order shown below. (20 pts)

6	1	7	10	5	8	4	9	3	2

2. Fill in the following blanks with 也 or 还. (4 pts).

1) 我有一只黑的狗，我__有一个白的狗。

2) 我有一支红铅笔，我弟弟__有一支红铅笔。

3. Fill in the blanks with appropriate measure words using 个 块 支 把 只. (16 pts)

1) 我有三＿咖啡色的铅笔，弟弟一＿咖啡色的铅笔也没有。

2) 我有一＿蓝的书包，弟弟也有一＿蓝的书包。

3) 弟弟有一＿黄苹果，我也有一＿黄苹果。

3) 这是什么？
这是一＿白板。

4) 那是什么？
那是一＿钥匙。

4. Negate the following sentences using 不，这不是....... (20 pts)

1) 这是你弟弟的狗吗？

_____。

2) 这是你的红苹果吗？

_____。

3) 这是弟弟的钥匙吗？

_____。

4) 这是你的铅笔吗？

_____。

5) 这个咖啡的书包是你的吗？

_____。

5. Match the following Chinese to their corresponding pinyin. (20 pts)

一只黑的狗	nǐ yǒu hēi de gǒu ma
我没有黑的狗	yī zhī hēi de gǒu
三个红苹果	wǒ méi yǒu hēi de gǒu
我有七只灰的猫	sān gè hóng píng guǒ
两只白的猫	liǎng zhī bái de māo
我没有狗没有猫	wǒ yǒu qī zhī huī de māo
你有黑的狗吗	sì gè lǜ píng guǒ
四个绿苹果	wǒ méi yǒu gǒu méi yǒu māo
这是什么	zhè bú shì dì di de shū bāo
这不是弟弟的书包	zhè shì shén me

6. Fill in the following blanks with 有 or 没有.
(10 pts)

我_____绿苹果(do not have)，我弟弟也

_____绿苹果。(does not have)

2) 我_____蓝的铅笔 (have)，我弟弟也

_____蓝的铅笔。(also has)

7. Fill in the following blanks with 也 or 还.
(10 points)

1) 弟弟有两个绿苹果，他__有两个红苹果。

2) 我弟弟有五个红苹果，我__有五个红苹果，我__有七个绿苹果。

第四课 问候?

复习 (Review)

1. Fill in the blanks in Chinese.

1) 你叫什么?

_____(My name is Arthur)。

2) 我叫Mary, 你呢?

_____ (My name is Mary too)。

3) 请进。

_____ (Thanks)。

_____ (You are welcome)。

2. Write the following numbers in Chinese in the exact same order shown below.

2	9	7	4	8	5	1	3	10	6

3. Fill in the blanks with appropriate measure words using 个 块 支 把 只.

1) 我有一＿黑板，我还有两＿蓝色的铅笔，一＿狗。

2) 这＿钥匙是你的吗?

3) 这＿书包是你的吗?
这＿＿书包不是我的，是Mary 的。

4. Fill in the following blanks with color words.

1) 弟弟有两个＿ (green)苹果，我也有两个＿ (green)苹果。

2) 哥哥的电脑是＿ (black)的，我的电脑是＿ (blue)的。

3) 我有三只＿ (gray)的狗，弟弟有三只 ＿ (white) 的猫。

4) 我的书包是＿ (red) 的，弟弟的书包是＿ (yellow)的。

5) 这个＿ (purple) 的铅笔是你的吗？
这是什么颜色？ 这是＿ (black) 的。 不是我的。

6) 这把＿＿＿＿ (brown) 钥匙是弟弟的，那个
＿＿＿＿ (orange) 的书包是Mary的。

5. Fill in the following blanks with 也 or 还.

1) 弟弟的铅笔是红的，我的铅笔＿是红的。
我有一个蓝的电脑，我弟弟＿有一个蓝的电
脑。

2) 这三个红苹果是弟弟的，这三个绿苹果＿
是弟弟的。

3) 弟弟有三支咖啡的铅笔，＿有个四支红铅
笔。

测验 (Quiz)

1. Count the squares below, and fill in the numbers in Chinese. (10 pts)

□□□□□ . □□□

(   ) + (   ) = (   )

2. Translate the following short dialogue into Chinese. (40 pts)

What's your name?

_____?

My name is Mary.

_____?

Come in, please.

_____.

Thanks.

_____.

You are welcome.

_____.

3. Fill in the following blanks in Chinese. (30 pts)

1) 弟弟有两个__ (red)苹果，我也有两个__ (red)苹果。

2) 哥哥的电脑是__ (blue)的，我的电脑是__ (black)的。

3) 我有三只＿ (white) 的猫，弟弟有三只＿ (gray) 的狗。

4) 我的书包是＿ (yellow) 的，弟弟的

书包是＿ (purple)的。

5) 这个＿＿＿＿(orange) 的铅笔是你的吗？

4. Negate the following sentences using 不，这不是……. (20 pts)

1) 这是你的书包吗？

＿＿＿＿＿＿＿＿＿＿＿＿。

2) 这是你的笔吗？

＿＿＿＿＿＿＿＿＿＿＿＿。

这只黑的狗是你弟弟的吗?

_____。

这是你哥哥的书包吗?

_____。

第五课 我的家

复习 (Review)

1. Answer the following questions in Chinese.

1) 你住在哪儿？

2) 你家的房子是什么颜色的？

3) 你家有没有花园？

4) 你家的大树在那儿？

5) 小松鼠在哪儿？

6) 你家有没有狗和猫?

7) 你家的狗叫什么?

8) 你家的猫叫什么?

2. Choose one appropriate word from the following list to correspond to what's mentioned in each of the sentences.

a. 边上 b. 白房子 c. 小松鼠 d. 花园
e. 一棵大树 f. 漂亮的 g. 只 h. 家
j. 谁的

1) Whose house is this white house?

_____

That's John's home.

_____

2) Whose garden is that?

_____

That is Tom's beautiful garden.

_____

3) Where is the little Squirrel?

_____

Over there. It's beside a big tree.

_____

3. Match the following Chinese to their corresponding pinyin.

我的家	piào liàng de huā yuán
有一个	hēi de māo
小松鼠	bái de gǒu
白的狗	yǒu yī kē dà shù
黑的猫	wǒ de jiā
这个白房子	zhè gè bái fáng zi
漂亮的花园	yǒu yī gè
有一棵大树	xiǎo sōng shǔ
大树边上有	dà shù biān shàng yǒu

4. Find the Chinese equivalents of the English words listed, and label them with the corresponding letters.

1) 那个漂亮的白房子是谁的家?

a. white house

b. beautiful

c. whose house

2) 我想这是Sam的家。

a. this is

b. home

c. I think

3) Sam家有一个漂亮的花园。 他家花园的边上有一棵大树。

a. a beautiful garden

b. next to

c. a big tree

4) 大树边上的那只漂亮的小黑猫是谁家的？

a. a black kitten

b. next to the big tree

c. whose

测验 (Quiz)

1. Write down the Chinese words you hear from the teacher. You can find the recording at www.PrincessImprints.com: Audio. (20 pts)

———————————

———————————

———————————

———————————

———————————

———————————

———————————

———————————

2. Fill in each blank with one appropriate choice from the following list. (20 pts)

a. 边上　b. 房子　c. 小松鼠　d.花园

e. 一棵　f. 漂亮　g. 只　h. 家　i. 叫

j. 花园里

1) 我家有一个＿＿＿＿＿＿的花园 。

2) ＿＿＿＿＿＿的＿＿＿＿＿＿有＿＿＿＿＿＿大树。

3) 那个白＿＿＿＿＿＿是我的＿＿＿＿＿＿。

4) 爷爷家的狗＿＿＿＿＿＿Nipper。

5) 大树上有两＿＿＿＿＿＿小＿＿＿＿＿＿。

6) ＿＿＿＿＿＿有两棵大树。

3. Answer the following questions in Chinese. (20 pts)

1) 你家的房子是什么颜色的？

2) 你住在哪儿？

3) 那个花园是谁家的？

4) 小松鼠在哪儿？

5) 爷爷家的狗叫什么？

4. Match the following Chinese to their corresponding pinyin. (20 pts)

这个白房子	yé ye jiā de gǒu
我的家	piào liàng de huā yuán
白的狗	hēi de māo
小松鼠	bái de gǒu
大树边上有	yǒu yī kē dà shù
黑的猫	wǒ de jiā
漂亮的花园	yǒu yī gè
有一棵大树	xiǎo sōng shǔ
有一个	dà shù biān shàng yǒu
爷爷家的狗	zhè gè bái fáng zi

5. Find the Chinese equivalents of the English words listed, and label them with the corresponding letters. (20 pts)

1) 那个漂亮的白房子是谁的家?

a. beautiful

b. white house

c. whose house

2) 我想这是Sam的家。

a. home

b. I think

c. this is

3) Sam家有一个漂亮的花园。 他家花园的边上有一棵大树。

a. next to

b. a beautiful garden

c. a big tree

4) 大树边上的那只漂亮的小黑猫是谁家的？

a. whose

b. next to the big tree

c. a black kitten

第六课 学校

复习 (Review)

1. Answer the following questions in Chinese.

1) 这栋红房子是谁的学校?

2) 你的教室在几楼?

3) 谁是你的老师?

4) 你的老师叫什么?

5) 你的好朋友叫什么? 他/她姓什么?

6) 他/她的老师是谁?

7) 他/她住在哪儿?

8) 他/她爸爸叫什么?

9) 他/她妈妈叫什么?

2. Fill in each blank with one appropriate choice from the following list.

a. 教室   b. 房子   c. 学校   d. 谁是

e. 一棵   f. 几楼   g. 姓   h. 同学   i. 叫

j. 边上

1) 那栋红＿＿＿＿是你的＿＿＿＿吗?

2) 你的＿＿＿＿在＿＿＿＿?

3) ＿＿＿＿你的＿＿＿＿?

4) 你的中文老师＿＿＿＿什么? 他/她＿＿＿＿什么?

5) 房子＿＿＿＿有＿＿＿＿大树。

3. Translate the following sentences into Chinese.

1) Whose school is this red house?

_____?

2) On which floor is your classroom?

_____。

3) What is your Chinese teacher's name?

_____?

4) Who is he?

_____?

He is my classmate.

_____。

His name is Alex.

_____ o

5) What is this?

_____?

This is a computer.

_____ o

6) What is that?

_____ o

That is a light.

_____ o

4. Match the following Chinese to their corresponding pinyin.

那栋红房子   wǒ de tóng xué

我的教室   nǐ de lǎo shī jiào shén me

在三楼   wǒ de jiào shì

这是谁   piào liang de xiào yuán

我的同学   nǐ de hǎo péng you jiào shén me

他叫什么   tā jiào shén me

他姓什么   shuí shì tā de Zhōng wén lǎo shī

你的老师叫什么   tā xìng shén me

谁是他的中文老师   zhè shì shuí

你的好朋友叫什么   zài sān lóu

漂亮的校园   nà dòng hóng fáng zi

5. Find the Chinese equivalents of the English words listed, and label them with the corresponding letters.

1) 那栋漂亮的红房子是我的学校。

a. that beautiful red building

b. my school

c. is

2) 我的教室在二楼。

a. the 2nd floor

b. my classroom

c. on

3) 你的中文老师叫什么？

a. your

b. what

c. Chinese teacher

4) 我的好朋友也是我妹妹的好朋友。

a. my good friend

b. my younger sister

c. is also

测验 (Quiz)

1. Write down the Chinese words you hear from the teacher. You can find the recording at www.PrincessImprints.com: Audio. (10 pts)

_____

_____

_____

_____

_____

_____

_____

_____

_____

2. Answer the following questions in Chinese. (30 pts)

1) 他是谁?

2) 谁是你的好朋友?

3) 你的中文老师是谁?

4) 你的英文老师是谁?

5) 你的教室在几楼?

6) 那栋红房子是你的学校吗?

7) Sam住在哪儿?

8) 这是什么?

9) 那是什么?

10) 你的同学Alex喜欢什么?

3. Fill in each blank with one appropriate choice from the following list. (20 pts)

a. 一棵   b. 老师   c. 学校   d. 几楼
e. 教室   f. 谁是   g. 房子   h. 边上   i. 叫

1) 房子_____有_____大树。

2) 你的_____在_____?

3) _____你的_____?

4) 你的中文老师_____什么?

5) 那栋红_____是你的_____吗?

4. Translate the following sentences into Chinese (20 pts).

1) Whose school is that white house?

_____?

2) What is Sam's classmate's name?

_____?

3) Sam's classroom is on the 3rd floor.

_____。

4) What is Chinese teacher's name?

_____?

5) What is this?

_____?

This is my home.

_____o

6) What is that?

_____?

That is my school.

_____o

7) He is my classmate, Sam.

_____o

8) Thank you. Bye.

_____o

5. Match the following Chinese to their corresponding pinyin (10 pts).

我的同学   nǐ de lǎo shī jiào shén me

在三楼   wǒ de tóng xué

这是谁   tā xǐ huān shén me

我的教室   wǒ de jiào shì

你的老师叫什么   piào liang de xiào yuán

他叫什么   tā jiào shén me

他喜欢什么   shuí shì tā de Zhōng wén lǎo shī

谁是他的中文老师   zhè shì shuí

那栋红房子   zài sān lóu

漂亮的校园   nà dòng hóng fáng zi

6. Find the Chinese equivalents of the English words listed, and label them with the corresponding letters. (10 pts)

1) 那栋漂亮的红房子是我的学校。

a. that beautiful red building

b. is

c. my school

2) 我的教室在二楼。

a. on

b. my classroom

c. the 2nd floor

3) 你的中文老师叫什么?

a. Chinese teacher

b. your

c. what

4) 我的好朋友也是我妹妹的好朋友。

a. my good friend

b. my younger sister

c. is also

第七课 今天几号？

复习 (Review)

1. Tell today's date using the following pattern.
Example:

今天是2013 年十月一号, 星期二。

2. Answer the following questions in Chinese.

1) 今天几号？

2) 今天星期几？

3) 明天几号？

4) 明天星期几?

5) 昨天呢?

6) 你喜欢看《超人》吗?

7) 下星期五晚上你做什么?

8) 在家看DVD有意思吗?

9) 你什么时候和你的同学一起去看电影?

10) 现在有什么新电影?

3. Fill in each blank with one appropriate choice from the following list.

a. 五月 b. 明天 c. 今天 d. 电影

e. 一起 f. 去看 g. 什么 h. 《超人》

i. 很有意思

1) 今天是_____三号，是吗？

2) _____几号？

3) _____你和谁_____ _____ ？

4) 你们昨天晚上你和谁在_____？

5) 这个电影_____。

6) 你昨天晚上和Robyn去看了_____电影？

_____吗？

4. Translate the following sentences into Chinese.

1) What is today's date?

_____?

2) On which floor is your classroom?

_____?

3) What is your Chinese teacher's name?

_____?

4) Today is Saturday, June 1, 2013.

_____。

5) Tomorrow is Sunday, June 2.

_____。

6) Tomorrow night I will go to watch a new movie with my classmate Sam. I heard this movie was very interesting.

_____。

7) I heard their garden was very beautiful.

_____。

5. Find the Chinese equivalents of the English words listed, and label them with the corresponding letters.

1) 今天是十二月十二号，明天是我妈妈的生日。

a. tomorrow

b. today is

c. December 12th

d. my mom's birthday

2) 我和Sam星期六一起去看电影。

a. go and watch movie

b. and

c. Saturday

d. together

3) 今天几号？

a. today

b. what

c. date

4) 我的生日是五月十五号，星期天

a. my birthday

b. Sunday

c. May 15th

测验 (Quiz)

1. Write down the Chinese words you hear from
the teacher. You can find the recording at
www.PrincessImprints.com: Audio. (20 pts)

_____

_____

_____

_____

_____

_____

_____

_____

2. Answer the following questions in Chinese. (30 pts)

1) 今天几号?

2) 今天星期几?

3) 昨天几号?

4) 昨天星期几?

5) 明天呢? 明天是五月八号吗?

6) 你的生日是几月几号?

7) 你好朋友的生日是几月几号?

8) 你和你的好朋友是什么时候去看电影的?

9) 你什么时候去好朋友的家?

10) 明天你做什么?

3. Fill in each blank with one appropriate choice from the following list. (10 pts)

a. 生日　b. 五月　c. 昨天　d. 星期六

e. 四号　f. 一起　g. 新电影　h. 星期天

i. 几月几号　j. 星期五

1) 今天是五月三号，明天是＿＿＿＿＿＿＿＿＿＿＿＿。

2) ＿＿＿＿＿＿是＿＿＿＿＿＿，今天是＿＿＿＿＿＿。

3) 你的生日是＿＿＿＿＿＿？

4) 昨天是＿＿＿＿＿＿，我和Sam＿＿＿＿＿＿去看了一个＿＿＿＿＿＿。

5) 你的＿＿＿＿＿＿是几月几号？

4. Translate the following sentences into Chinese. (20 pts)

1) What is today's date?

_____?

2) Today is Wednesday, May 5.

_____?

3) What is the date of tomorrow?

_____?

4) When are you going to watch the new movie with Sam?

_____?

5) When is your sister's birthday?

_____?

5. Match the following Chinese to their corresponding pinyin. (10 pts)

很有意思　　　　　　　　wǔ yuè shí bā hào shì Xīng qí jǐ

去看一个新电影　　　　　zuó tiān shì sān yuè shí yī hào

今天几号　　　　　　　　jīn nián shí èr yuè shí èr hào

明天是星期天　　　　　　nǐ de shēng rì shì jǐ yuè jǐ hào

六月二号星期三　　　　　jīn tiān jǐ hào

你的生日是几月几号　　　hěn yǒu yì si

他的生日是三月三号　　　míng tiān shì Xīng qí tiān

今年十二月十二号　　　　liù yuè èr hào Xīng qí sān

五月十八号是星期几　　　qù kàn yī gè xīn diàn yǐng

昨天是三月十一号　　　　tā de shēng rì shì sān yuè sān hào

6. Find the Chinese equivalents of the English words listed, and label them with the corresponding letters. (10 pts)

1) 今天几号？

a. today

b. what

c. date

2) 我的生日是五月十五号，星期天。

a. my birthday

b. Sunday

c. May 15th

3) 我和Sam星期六一起去看电影。

a. Saturday

b. and

c. go and watch movie

d. together

4) 今天是十二月十二号，我妈妈的生日是明天。

a. my mom's birthday

b. today is

c. December 12th

d. tomorrow

第八课 现在几点?

复习 (Review)

1. Answer the following questions in Chinese.

1) 现在几点?

2) 你每天几点上学?

3) 你每天几点放学?

4) 你每天几点吃午饭?

5) 你的中文课是星期三下午几点?

6) 你昨天下午几点打电话给你妈妈的?

7) 你星期六上午几点去上中文课?

8) 你们明天几点去Sam家玩?

2. Fill in each blank with one appropriate choice
from the following list.

a. 几点　b. 每天　c. 七点　d.上午

e. 星期几　f. 晚上　g. 下午　h. 三点一刻

i. 九点　j. 十二点　k. 十点半

1) 现在是_____吗？

2) 现在_____?

3) 你们明天_____几点去Sam家玩?

4) 我每天差不多_____吃午饭。

5) 你_____几点上课？

6) 你的好朋友是明天下午_____来你家玩
吗？

7) 你的好朋友是昨天晚上_____来你家的吗?

8) 我爸爸明天上午_____去中国。

9) 我和Sam每天_____学习中文。

10) 你妈妈是_____ _____三点去美国的?

3. Translate the following sentences into Chinese.

1) What time is it now?

_____?

It is 3:15.

_____。

2) When will your mom go to China?

_____?

She is going to China on Thursday night at 7:30.

_____.

3) Are you going to China with your mom?

_____?

No. I will go to China with my dad on Saturday night at 7:45.

_____.

4) What time do you go to school everyday?

_____?

I go to school at 7:30 in the morning.

_____.

5) When is the school over everyday?

_____?

Two thirty in the afternoon.

_____.

4. Match the following Chinese to their corresponding pinyin.

现在几点   nǐ měi tiān jǐ diǎn xià kè

你每天上午几点上课   xiàn zài jǐ diǎn

你几点去图书馆   wǒ jiǔ diǎn yī kè lái

我是下午三点去的   měi tiān xià wǔ liǎng diǎn bàn

你明天什么时候来   nǐ mèi mei yě lái ma

我九点一刻来   nǐ bà ba zuó tiān jǐ diǎn huí qù de

你妹妹也来吗   tā wǎn shàng qī diǎn lái

她晚上七点来   nǐ míng tiān shén me shí hou lái

你每天几点下课   wǒ shì xià wǔ sān diǎn qù de

每天下午两点半   nǐ jǐ diǎn qù tú shū guǎn

你爸爸昨天几点回去的   nǐ měi tiān shàng wǔ jǐ diǎn shàng kè

5. Find the Chinese equivalents of the English words listed, and label them with the corresponding letters.

1) 你星期六上午几点上中文课?

a. on Saturday morning

b. have Chinese lessons

c. what time

2) 你昨天下午几点去Sam家的?

a. yesterday afternoon

b. went to Sam's house

c. what time

3) 你每天几点去上学?

a. go to school

b. what time

c. everyday

4) 我每天晚上六点半去图书馆。

a. go to library

b. six thirty

c. every evening

测验 (Quiz)

1. Write down the Chinese words you hear from the teacher. You can find the recording at www.PrincessImprints.com: Audio. (10 pts)

_____

_____

_____

_____

_____

_____

_____

_____

_____

2. Answer the following questions in Chinese. (30 pts)

1) 现在几点?

2) 你昨天下午几点打电话给你妈妈的?

3) 你每天几点上学?

4) 你们明天几点去Sam家玩?

5) 你每天几点吃午饭?

6) 你星期六上午几点去上中文课?

7) 你每天几点放学?

8) 你的中文课是星期三上午几点?

9) 你明天几点上英文课?

10) 你爸爸今天几点回家?

3. Fill in each blank with one appropriate choice from the following list. (20 pts)

a. 下午　b. 晚上　c. 七点　d. 九点

e. 星期几　f. 每天　g. 几点　h. 三点一刻

i. 上午　j. 十点半　k. 十二点

1) 现在是_____吗？

2) 现在_____？

3) 你们明天_____几点去Sam家玩?

4) 我每天差不多_____吃午饭。

5) 你_____几点上学?

6) 你的好朋友是明天下午_____

来你家玩吗？

7) 你的好朋友是昨天晚上_____来你家的吗?

8) 我爸爸明天上午_____去中国。

9) 我和Sam每天_____ _____学习中文。

10) 你妈妈是_____ _____三点去美国的?

4．Translate the following sentences into Chinese. (20 pts)

1) What time is it now?

_____?

It is 12:15PM.

_____.

2) Are you going to China with Sam's mom?

_____?

Yes.

_____.

3) What time is your mom going to China?

_____.

Tomorrow afternoon.

_____?

4) I will go to China with my dad on Saturday night at 7:45.

_____.

5) What time do you go to school everyday?

_____?

I go to school at 7:30 in the morning.

_____.

6) What time do you get out of the school everyday?

_____?

Two thirty in the afternoon.

_____.

5. Match the following Chinese to their corresponding pinyin. (10 pts)

现在几点   nǐ jǐ diǎn qù tú shū guǎn

你每天上午几点上课   xiàn zài jǐ diǎn

你几点去图书馆   wǒ jiǔ diǎn yī kè lái

我是下午三点去的   nǐ míng tiān shén me shí hou lái

你明天什么时候来   nǐ mèi mei yě lái ma

我九点一刻来   nǐ zuó tiān jǐ diǎn huí qù de

你妹妹也来吗   tā wǎn shàng qī diǎn lái

她晚上七点来   měi tiān xià wǔ liǎng diǎn bàn

你每天几点下课   wǒ shì xià wǔ sān diǎn qù de

每天下午两点半   nǐ měi tiān jǐ diǎn xià kè

你昨天几点回去的   nǐ měi tiān shàng wǔ jǐ diǎn shàng kè

5. Find the Chinese equivalents of the English words listed, and label them with the corresponding letters. (10 pts)

1) 你是昨天下午三点去Sam家的?

a. went to

b. yesterday afternoon

c. Sam's house

2) 你星期二上午几点上中文课?

a. on Tuesday morning

b. what time

c. have Chinese lesson

3) 你每天几点上英文课？

a. have English class
b. everyday
c. what time

4) 我每天晚上六点半去图书馆。

a. go to library
b. six thirty
c. every evening

第九课 天气

复习 (Review)

1. Answer the following questions in Chinese.

1) 今天天好吗?

2) 今天上午天晴吗?

3) 明天什么时候下雨?

4) 明天天好吗?

5) 听说明天上午要下雪，是吗?

6) 是谁说今天多云，但是不下雨?

7) 明天多云吗?

8) 听说明天上午刮风，下午下雪，是吗?

9) 昨天天不好，又下雨，又下雪。

2. Fill in each blank with one appropriate choice from the following list.

a. 天气 b. 下雪 c. 怎么样 d.刮风

e. 晴天 f. 风很大 g. 没风 h. 外面很冷

i. 很热

1) 明天_____ _____?
明天不下雨, 可是明天_____。

2) 今天_____吗?
今天不刮风，可是_____。

3) 今天热不热?
今天_____, _____。

4) 明天天好吗?
明天_____, 可是_____。

3. Translate the following sentences into Chinese.

1) What is the weather like today?

_____?

2) What was the weather like yesterday?

_____?

3) It is a nice day today, but I heard it will be raining tomorrow.

_____。

4) It is raining, snowing, and windy.

_____。

5) It's neither cold nor hot, very comfortable.

_____。

6) It is hot in the morning, but it will cool down in the afternoon.

_____o

7) It is cold outside.

_____o

8) I heard tomorrow afternoon will be very, very cold.

_____o

9) Tomorrow will be a little better.

_____o

10) It's a nice day today, isn't it?

_____?

4. Match the following Chinese to their corresponding pinyin.

今天天很好	jīn tiān qíng tiān
明天很冷，要下雪	míng tiān tiān hěn hǎo
今天下午刮风下雨	jīn tiān tiān hěn lěng
明天天气怎么样	tīng shuō míng tiān yào xià xuě
明天天很好	jīn tiān tiān hěn rè
今天晴天	jīn tiān duō yún
今天没雨	míng tiān tiān qì zěn me yàng
听说明天要下雪	míng tiān hěn lěng, yào xià xuě
今天天很冷	jīn tiān xià wǔ guā fēng xià yǔ
今天天很热	jīntiān méi yǔ
今天多云	jīn tiān tiān hěn hǎo

5. Find the Chinese equivalents of the English words listed, and label them with the corresponding letters.

1) 明天是星期六，要下雨。

a. will be raining

b. tomorrow

c. Saturday

2) 明天天气怎么样？

a. tomorrow

b. how

c. weather

3) 今天下午又刮风，又下雨。

a. this afternoon

b. raining

c. windy

4) 今天天很好，可是，明天要下雪。

a. will be snowing

b. but

c. today is a very nice day

测验 (Quiz)

1. Write down the Chinese words you hear from the teacher. You can find the recording at www.PrincessImprints.com: Audio. (10 pts)

_____

_____

_____

_____

_____

_____

_____

_____

2. Answer the following questions in Chinese. (20 pts)

1) 听说明天上午多云，下午下雪，是吗？

2) 明天天好吗？

3) 听说明天上午要下雪，是吗？

4) 是谁说今天不下雨，今天刮风？

5) 明天多云吗？

6) 今天天好吗？

7) 明天不好，又下雨，又下雪。

8) 今天上午天晴吗？

9) 明天什么时候下雨？

3. Fill in each blank with one appropriate choice from the following list. (20 pts)

a. 九点 b. 每天 c. 七点 d. 下午

e. 上午 f. 晚上 g. 几点 h. 十二点

i. 星期几 j. 十点半 k. 三点一刻

1) 现在是_____吗?

2) 现在_____?

3) 你们明天_____几点去Sam家玩?

4) 我每天差不多_____吃午饭。

5) 你_____几点上学?

6) 你的好朋友是明天下午_____

来你家玩吗?

7) 你的好朋友是昨天晚上_____来你家的吗?

8) 我爸爸明天上午_____去中国。

9) 我和Sam每天_____学习中文。

10) 你妈妈是_____ _____三点去美国的?

4. Translate the following sentences into Chinese. (20 pts)

1) What is the weather like tomorrow?

_____?

 2) It is windy and cold today.

_____。

3) I heard it is going to snow in the afternoon.

_____。

4) Tomorrow is very hot, are you still going to New York?

_____?

5) This morning is sunny, but it is going to rain in the afternoon.

_____。

6) There will be no rain tomorrow.

_____?

7) What is the weather like today in New York?

_____?

8) If tomorrow is not raining, we'll go to New York.

_____?

9) Tomorrow is a very nice day.

_____。

10) I heard it will be raining and snowing tomorrow afternoon.

_____。

5. Match the following Chinese to their corresponding pinyin. (10 pts)

今天天很好　　　　　　　tīng shuō míng tiān yào xià xuě

明天很冷，要下雪　　　　míng tiān tiān hěn hǎo

今天下午刮风下雨　　　　jīn tiān tiān hěn lěng

明天天气怎么样　　　　　jīn tiān qíng tiān

明天天很好　　　　　　　jīn tiān tiān hěn rè

今天晴天　　　　　　　　jīn tiān tiān hěn hǎo

今天没雨　　　　　　　　míng tiān tiān qì zěn me yàng

听说明天要下雪　　　　　jīn tiān méi yǔ

今天天很冷　　　　　　　jīn tiān xià wǔ guā fēng xià yǔ

今天天很热　　　　　　　míng tiān hěn lěng, yào xià xuě

今天多云　　　　　　　　jīn tiān duō yún

6. Find the Chinese equivalents of the English words listed, and label them with the corresponding letters. (20 pts)

1) 听说明天下午要下雪。

a. heard

b. tomorrow afternoon

c. is going to snow

2) 昨天晚上又刮风又下雨

a. night

b. yesterday

c. windy and rainy

3) 明天天气怎么样?

a. how

b. weather

c. tomorrow

4) 今天上午是晴天，可是，下午多云。

a. sunny

b. this morning

c. but

d. cloudy in the afternoon

第十课 家庭和朋友

复习 (Review)

1. Answer the following questions in Chinese.

你家有几口人?

他们是谁?

你们住在哪儿?

你爷爷奶奶家住在哪儿?

你爸爸有妹妹吗?

你爸爸的妹妹叫什么?

你妈妈有几个姐姐?

你的好朋友Sam住在哪儿?

谁住在纽约?

2. Fill in each blank with one appropriate choice from the following list.

a. 爸爸　b. 妈妈　c. 哥哥　d. 在

e. 几口　f. 谁　g. 姐姐　h. 费城

i. 哪儿　j. 住在

1) 你家有_____人?

2) 你_____哪儿?

3) 你爷爷奶奶家在_____?

4) 你好朋友Sam的_____叫什么?

5) 你好朋友Sam家都有_____?

6) 我住在纽约，你住在_____吗?

7) 你外公外婆家_____哪儿?

8) 我家有四口人：_____、_____、_____和我。

3. Translate the following dialogue into Chinese.

1) Where do you live?

_____?

I live in Philadelphia. And you?

_____?

I live in New York with my mom and dad.

_____。

2) How many people are there in your family?

_____?

Six.

_____。

Who are they?

_____?

My dad, mom, one elder brother, two younger sisters and I.

_____。

3) I heard your grandpa and grandma live in New York.

_____。

No, they live in Philadelphia.

_____。

4. Match the following Chinese to their corresponding pinyin.

你家有几口人	wǒ men dōu xǐ huan Niǔyuē
你住在哪儿	wǒ wài gōng wài pó zhù zài Niǔyue
你爷爷家在哪儿	yī gè xìng fú de dà jiā tíng
纽约人多不多	wǒ jiā yǒu hěn duō péng you
你喜欢纽约吗	wǒ de hǎo péng you zhù zài Fèi chéng
我的好朋友住在费城	nǐ xǐ huan Niǔ yuē ma
我家有很多朋友	nǐ yé ye jiā zài nǎ'er
我外公外婆住在纽约	nǐ jiā yǒu jǐ kǒu rén
我们都喜欢纽约	Niǔ yuē rén duō bù duō
一个幸福的大家庭	nǐ zhù zài nǎ'er

5. Find the Chinese equivalents of the English words listed, and label them with the corresponding letters.

1) 我家有七口人。

a. there are

b. my family

c. seven people

2) 我有一个幸福的大家庭。

a. big family

b. happy

c. I have a

3) 我爷爷奶奶住在纽约。

a. New York

b. my grandpa and grandma

c. live

4) 我的好朋友住在费城。

a. lives

b. Philadelphia

c. my good friend

测验 (Quiz)

1. Write down the Chinese words you hear from the teacher. You can find the recording at www.PrincessImprints.com: Audio. (20 pts)

_____

_____

_____

_____

_____

_____

_____

_____

_____

3. Fill in each blank with one appropriate choice from the following list. (20 pts)

a. 爸爸   b. 住在   c. 几口   d. 在
e. 哥哥   f. 谁   g. 姐姐   h. 哪儿
i. 费城   j. 妈妈

1) 你家有_____人?

2) 你_____哪儿?

3) 你爷爷奶奶家在_____?

4) 你好朋友Sam的_____叫什么?

5) 你好朋友Sam家都有_____?

6) 我住在纽约，你住在_____吗?

7) 你外公外婆家_____哪儿?

8) 我家有四口人: _____、_____、
_____和我。

4. Translate the following sentences into Chinese. (20 pts)

1) Where do your live?

_____?

2) My parents live in Philadelphia.

_____。

3) Sam lives in New York with his younger sister.

_____。

4) How many people are there in Sam's family?

_____?

There are eleven people in Sam's family.

_____。

5. Match the following Chinese to their corresponding pinyin (20 pts).

你家有几口人　　　　　　wǒ men dōu xǐ huan Niǔ yuē

你住在哪儿　　　　　　　wǒ wài gōng wài pó zhù zài Niǔ yue

你爷爷家在哪儿　　　　　yī gè xìng fú de dà jiā tíng

纽约人多不多　　　　　　wǒ jiā yǒu hěn duō péng you

你喜欢纽约吗　　　　　　wǒ de hǎo péng you zhù zài Fèi chéng

我的好朋友住在费城　　　nǐ xǐ huan Niǔ yuē ma

我家有很多朋友　　　　　nǐ yéye jiā zài nǎ'er

我外公外婆住在纽约　　　nǐ jiā yǒu jǐ kǒu rén

我们都喜欢纽约　　　　　Niǔ yuē rén duō bù duō

一个幸福的大家庭　　　　nǐ zhù zài nǎ'er

5. Find the Chinese equivalents of the English words listed, and label them with the corresponding letters. (20 pts)

1) 他家有六口人。

a. six people

b. his family has

c. six people

2) 她有一个幸福的小家庭。

a. small family

b. happy

c. she has

3) 他的女朋友住在费城。

a. in Philadelphia

b. lives

c. his girl friend

4) 我的好朋友住在纽约。

a. lives

b. New York

c. my good friend

Chinese as a Foreign Language Textbooks Written *by* Bill Li
Illustrations by Candace Tong-Li

Chinese for Young Beginners 1 (Chinese-English Edition)

Chinese for Young Beginners 2 (Chinese-English Edition)

Chinese for Young Beginners 3 (Chinese-English Edition)

Picture Books Written and Illustrated *by* Candace Tong-Li
Chinese Translations by Bill Li

Baby Crane and Other Animal Tales (Chinese Edition, Age 4-10)

Acorn and Katie (Chinese-English Edition, Age 4-8)

The Moon Stallion (Chinese-English Edition, Age 4-8)

Snow Dogs (Chinese-English Edition, Age 4-10)

Snow Leopard (Chinese-English Edition, Age 4-10)

Tales of Titans - Timeless Dinosaur Stories (English Edition, Age 6-12)

The Puppy Prince (English and Chinese-English Editions, Age 2-5)

New York

Imagine. Create. Contribute.

www.PrincessImprints.com

Email: ChineseTutor@PrincessImprints.com

Printed in U.S.A.